# DREN CHED

## STUDY GUIDE

For foreign and subsidiary rights, contact the author.

Cover design by: Sara Young
Cover photo by: Raven Cannon

ISBN: 978-1-962401-10-4     1 2 3 4 5 6 7 8 9 10

Printed in the United States of America

Thoroughly Covered and Completely Filled

# DRENCHED

## JEFF STANFORD

### STUDY GUIDE

ARROWS & STONES

# CONTENTS

Thoroughly Covered and Completely Filled

# DRENCHED

## JEFF STANFORD

*Forewords by Tony Stewart & Toby Morgan*

# THE DRENCHED LIFE

*The more sensitive you are to Him and follow His commands and counsel, the stronger, more stable, powerful, and victorious you will become.*

# REVIEW, REFLECT, AND RESPOND

## READING TIME

As you read Chapter 1 "The Drenched Life" in *Drenched*, review, reflect on, and respond to the text by answering the following questions.

Do you have a relationship with the Holy Spirit? Why or why not?

_____

_____

_____

_____

_____

_____

Which of the three baptisms (of salvation, in water, and in the Holy Spirit) have you received?

_____

_____

_____

_____

_____

_____

What have you learned, either growing up or presently, about being baptized in the Holy Spirit? Is it a positive thing? A scary thing? A weird thing?

_____

_____

_____

_____

_____

_____

*And it shall come to pass in the last days, saith God, I will pour out of my Spirit upon all flesh: and your sons and your daughters shall prophesy, and your young men shall see visions, and your old men shall dream dreams: And on my servants and on my handmaidens I will pour out in those days of my Spirit; and they shall prophesy.*

—Acts 2:17-18 (KJV)

*Consider the scripture above and answer the following questions:*

What conclusions can you draw from this promise about the person of the Holy Spirit?

_____

_____

_____

_____

_____

_____

_____

How willing are you to let the rain of the Holy Spirit fall on you? Why?

_____

_____

_____

_____

_____

_____

_____

Have you ever asked God for the baptism of the Holy Spirit?

_____

_____

_____

_____

_____

_____

If you were to ask God for Him to show you what it means to be drenched in the Spirit, what would you say?

_____

_____

_____

_____

_____

_____

In what ways do you think being completely filled with the Holy Spirit would affect your walk with God?

_____

_____

_____

_____

_____

_____

# COMMUNION WITH THE HOLY SPIRIT

*As you are gracious to others, loving others, especially the unlovable, it keeps you in fellowship with the Holy Spirit.*

READING
TIME

As you read
Chapter 2:
"Communion
With the
Holy Spirit"
in *Drenched*,
review, reflect
on, and respond
to the text by
answering
the following
questions.

# REVIEW, REFLECT, AND RESPOND

What can you draw from Paul's advice in this chapter about staying in the grace of Jesus Christ to remain in communion with the Holy Spirit?

_____

_____

_____

_____

_____

What do you think it means to stay in God's grace? Why do you think it is necessary in order to fellowship with the Holy Spirit?

_____

_____

_____

_____

_____

How does knowing God's insistence on building an indestructible relationship with you change the way you view the person of the Holy Spirit?

_____

_____

_____

_____

_____

> *The love of God is shed abroad in our hearts*
> *by the Holy Ghost which is given to us.*
>
> —Romans 5:5 (KJV)

*Consider the scripture above and answer the following questions:*

What do you think the role of love is in cultivating a relationship with the Holy Spirit?

_____

_____

_____

_____

_____

_____

_____

_____

How do you think the love of God and culture's definition of love differ from one another?

_____

_____

_____

_____

_____

_____

_____

_____

Do you think you are in complete partnership with the Holy Spirit? How do you know?

_____

_____

_____

_____

_____

_____

_____

What do you think the Holy Spirit can teach us about intimacy that we wouldn't learn otherwise without Him?

_____

_____

_____

_____

_____

_____

_____

Of the seven meanings of communion listed in this chapter (presence, fellowship, sharing together, participation, intimacy, friendship, commander), which are you least familiar with? Which are you most familiar with?

_____

_____

_____

_____

_____

_____

_____

# UNDER THE INFLUENCE

*I believe God is—right now—pouring out His Holy Spirit on those who are hungry, thirsty, and available for more of Him in their lives.*

# REVIEW, REFLECT, AND RESPOND

## READING TIME

As you read
Chapter 3:
"Under the
Influence"
in *Drenched*,
review, reflect
on, and respond
to the text by
answering
the following
questions.

Thinking about the example of intoxication, what do you think being drunk in the Holy Spirit feels like or looks like?

_____

_____

_____

_____

_____

_____

Considering the gospels, in what ways can you observe and recognize Holy Spirit intoxication in Jesus?

_____

_____

_____

_____

_____

_____

What steps are you taking or have you taken to reach the place of being under the influence of the Holy Spirit?

_____

_____

_____

_____

_____

_____

> *On the last day, that great day of the feast, Jesus stood and cried out, saying, "If anyone thirsts, let him come to Me and drink. He who believes in Me, as the Scripture has said, out of his heart will flow rivers of living water." But this He spoke concerning the Spirit, whom those believing in Him would receive; for the Holy Spirit was not yet given because Jesus was not yet glorified.*
>
> —John 7:37-39 (NKJV)

*Consider the scripture above and answer the following questions:*

How do you know when you have drunk the living water? How will you know when you are no longer thirsting?

_____

_____

_____

_____

_____

_____

_____

_____

In what ways do you think rivers of living water flowing from the heart depict drunkenness in the Spirit?

_____

_____

_____

_____

_____

_____

_____

If you have not yet experienced what it is like to be under the influence of the Holy Spirit, what steps could you take today to experience it?

_____

_____

_____

_____

_____

_____

_____

How can you share the gift of Holy Spirit intoxication with others?

_____

_____

_____

_____

_____

_____

In what ways can you relate to the five characteristics of the drunk man described in this chapter? Which of these do you struggle relating to?

_____

_____

_____

_____

_____

_____

_____

# SUPER FRUITFUL

*The fruit of the Spirit is produced by the
Holy Spirit, not by the believer.*

# REVIEW, REFLECT, AND RESPOND

As you read
Chapter 4:
"Super Fruitful"
in *Drenched*,
review, reflect
on, and respond
to the text by
answering
the following
questions.

In what ways do you think your life is a manifestation of the Spirit's filling? In what ways is it not?

_____

_____

_____

_____

_____

Can you think of a time when you gave in to the force opposing the Holy Spirit? How did it impede your ability to produce the fruit of the Spirit?

_____

_____

_____

_____

_____

Of the nine characteristics of the fruit of the Spirit listed in this chapter (love, joy, peace, patience, kindness and goodness, faithfulness, gentleness and meekness, and self-control), which stands out to you as needing the most work?

_____

_____

_____

_____

_____

> *So I say, let the Holy Spirit guide your lives. Then you won't be doing what your sinful nature craves. The sinful nature wants to do evil, which is just the opposite of what the Spirit wants. And the Spirit gives us desires that are the opposite of what the sinful nature desires. These two forces are constantly fighting each other, so you are not free to carry out your good intentions. But when you are directed by the Spirit, you are not under obligation to the law of Moses.*
>
> —Galatians 5:16-18 (NLT)

*Consider the scripture above and answer the following questions:*

In what areas of your life have you allowed your sinful nature to win against the Holy Spirit?

_____

_____

_____

_____

_____

_____

When have you allowed the Holy Spirit to direct and control your life? What was that experience like, and how could you replicate it?

_____

_____

_____

_____

_____

_____

How have past attempts to produce fruitfulness apart from God's help ended? What were the results?

_____

_____

_____

_____

_____

_____

_____

How does developing credibility with the Holy Spirit bleed over into our everyday lives as witnesses of the power of the gospel?

_____

_____

_____

_____

_____

_____

What have you noticed in your own life about producing supernatural fruitfulness as a continuous, ongoing process?

_____

_____

_____

_____

_____

_____

_____

# SUPERNATURAL LANGUAGES AND OTHER GIFTS

*The Holy Spirit will give you the utterances, but He will not speak them for you. You must yield and speak forth the words as He gives them.*

As you read
Chapter 5:
"Supernatural
Languages and
Other Gifts"
in *Drenched*,
review, reflect
on, and respond
to the text by
answering
the following
questions.

# REVIEW, REFLECT, AND RESPOND

Have you received your spiritual language?
How often do you practice it during your
quiet time with the Lord?

_____

_____

_____

_____

_____

_____

Why do you think speaking in your prayer
language is self-edifying?

_____

_____

_____

_____

_____

What have you learned, perhaps before
reading this book, about speaking in
unknown tongues? What were your initial
impressions of it? How have they changed?

_____

_____

_____

_____

_____

_____

> *Likewise the Spirit also helpeth our infirmities: for we know not what we should pray for as we ought: but the Spirit itself maketh intercession for us with groanings which cannot be uttered. And he that searcheth the hearts knoweth what is the mind of the Spirit because he maketh intercession for the saints according to the will of God.*
>
> —Romans 8:26-27 (KJV)

*Consider the scripture above and answer the following questions:*

When prayer is hard, how do you stay in communication with God? In what ways do you withdraw from Him during those times?

_____

_____

_____

_____

_____

_____

_____

_____

How does this scripture lend to your understanding of the fullness and multi-dimensional person of the Holy Spirit?

_____

_____

_____

_____

_____

_____

_____

Why do you think it is so important that God has given us a way to reach Him when we aren't sure how to?

_____

_____

_____

_____

_____

_____

How is our prayer language evidence that we cannot live a life of strong character and uncompromising values without help beyond our own strength?

_____

_____

_____

_____

_____

_____

How do the answers provided in "Pressing Questions" in this chapter help you understand the Holy Spirit and the gift of tongues more clearly?

_____

_____

_____

_____

_____

_____

# THE SECRET CODE

*When we allow the Holy Spirit to pray, He always knows exactly what to say to our heavenly Father on our behalf.*

## READING TIME

As you read Chapter 6: "The Secret Code" in *Drenched*, review, reflect on, and respond to the text by answering the following questions.

# REVIEW, REFLECT, AND RESPOND

How do you understand the intercession of the Holy Spirit as a secret code that unlocks the answers to the deepest desires of our hearts?

_____

_____

_____

_____

_____

What do you imagine when you think about the Holy Spirit going *with* you to the Father as you present your needs to Him? Why is that so meaningful and valuable?

_____

_____

_____

_____

_____

Can you think of a time when God blessed you with something you didn't even know you needed? What can you glean from that experience as it relates to the intercession of the Holy Spirit?

_____

_____

_____

_____

_____

> *Call to Me, and I will answer you, and show you great and mighty things, which you do not know.*
>
> —Jeremiah 33:3 (NIV)

*Consider the scripture above and answer the following questions:*

How comfortable are you with calling on the Holy Spirit to show you what you do not know? What do you think holds you back?

_____

_____

_____

_____

_____

_____

_____

_____

What would it be like to expect God to show you "great and mighty things" that you could have never conceived of?

_____

_____

_____

_____

_____

_____

_____

_____

How does the Holy Spirit, as the advocate for our needs, known and unknown, impact your understanding of unexpected disappointments and valleys?

_____

_____

_____

_____

_____

_____

_____

In what ways have you experienced a decline in your desire to pray?

_____

_____

_____

_____

_____

_____

Why do you think reliance on our own limited knowledge of our needs blinds us to the needs of others?

_____

_____

_____

_____

_____

_____

_____

# YOUR HOLY TOUR GUIDE

*The Bible teaches us that life is a journey, and God has given us a roadmap for life. The Bible is our roadmap.*

As you read
Chapter 7:
"Your Holy
Tour Guide"
in *Drenched*,
review, reflect
on, and respond
to the text by
answering
the following
questions.

# REVIEW, REFLECT, AND RESPOND

What kind of things has the Holy Spirit protected you from that would have brought great harm to you?

_____

_____

_____

_____

_____

What kind of paths has the Holy Spirit guided you on that you otherwise would not have taken on your own?

_____

_____

_____

_____

_____

_____

How do you reconcile the tension between feeling like you are heading in an unknown direction and knowing that the Spirit knows exactly where He wants you to land?

_____

_____

_____

_____

_____

_____

*Consider the scripture above and answer the following questions:*

Why do you think it takes humility to be led and guided by the Holy Spirit?

_____

_____

_____

_____

_____

_____

_____

_____

What have you learned about His ways from times when you allowed the Spirit to teach you and direct you?

_____

_____

_____

_____

_____

_____

_____

_____

_____

What kind of dangers might you encounter if you disconnected from the Holy Spirit?

_____

_____

_____

_____

_____

_____

_____

What has happened when you attempted to walk along your path and take matters into your own hands in the past?

_____

_____

_____

_____

_____

_____

In what ways is your Tour Guide a protector?

_____

_____

_____

_____

_____

_____

_____

# YOU ARE NEVER ALONE

*Everywhere you go, and every moment of every day and every night, the Holy Spirit is always with you.*

READING
TIME

As you read
Chapter 8:
"You Are
Never Alone"
in *Drenched*,
review, reflect
on, and respond
to the text by
answering
the following
questions.

# REVIEW, REFLECT, AND RESPOND

In what ways have you felt disconnected or distanced from the Holy Spirit in the past? What did that feel like?

_____

_____

_____

_____

_____

_____

What do you think it means to "walk in the Spirit"? Describe a time when you felt the most connected to the Spirit.

_____

_____

_____

_____

_____

_____

_____

How does the continuous presence of the Holy Spirit release you from fear?

_____

_____

_____

_____

_____

_____

> *Don't be misled—you cannot mock the justice of God.*
> *You will always harvest what you plant. Those who live*
> *only to satisfy their sinful nature will harvest decay and*
> *death from that sinful nature. But those who live to please*
> *the Spirit will harvest everlasting life from the Spirit.*
>
> —Galatians 6:7-8 (NLT)

*Consider the scripture above and answer the following questions:*

Think of the biggest spiritual harvest you have ever reaped. What did your walk with the Holy Spirit look like at the time? How could you create more of those "harvest" moments?

_____

_____

_____

_____

_____

_____

_____

What do you think the Spirit finds pleasing as you acknowledge His presence each day?

_____

_____

_____

_____

_____

_____

_____

How much time are you making for God every day? What does your time with Him entail?

_____

_____

_____

_____

_____

_____

_____

_____

If you were to ask God whether He felt like He was getting enough of your attention, what do you think He would say?

_____

_____

_____

_____

_____

_____

Do you find it difficult to hear the voice of God? Why or why not?

_____

_____

_____

_____

_____

_____

_____

# THE WORSHIPERS

*One of the greatest responsibilities of every
born-again, Holy Spirit-filled believer is to
worship God in spirit and in truth.*

## READING TIME

As you read
Chapter 9: "The
Worshipers"
in *Drenched*,
review, reflect
on, and respond
to the text by
answering
the following
questions.

# REVIEW, REFLECT, AND RESPOND

What does your worship life look like these days? In what ways are you praising His name with regularity?

_____

_____

_____

_____

_____

_____

In what ways would you like to have a more vibrant, fulfilling life of worship? How could you get there?

_____

_____

_____

_____

_____

_____

Do you ever find worship to be challenging? When and why?

_____

_____

_____

_____

_____

_____

> *Let us worship and bow down. Let us kneel before the Lord our maker, for he is our God. We are the people he watches, over the flock under his care.*
>
> —Psalm 95:6-7 (NLT)

*Consider the scripture above and answer the following questions:*

Why do you think there is power in bowing down as you worship? What does it communicate to God?

_____

_____

_____

_____

_____

_____

_____

When do you tend to worship the most: when life is going well or when you are in desperate need of the hand of God?

_____

_____

_____

_____

_____

_____

_____

Why does thanking and praising God regardless of our circumstances move heaven?

_____

_____

_____

_____

_____

_____

What do you think your future would look like if you demanded your way? Why?

_____

_____

_____

_____

_____

_____

_____

_____

What kind of worshiper do you want to be? How satisfied are you with the way you worship God?

_____

_____

_____

_____

_____

_____

_____

# YOUR OWN PERSONAL TRAINER

*God also has a fitness program and plan to help everyone who serves Him. God has provided for us our very own personal trainer to help us be conformed to the image of Jesus Christ.*

READING
TIME

As you read
Chapter 10:
"Your Own
Personal
Trainer" in
*Drenched*,
review, reflect
on, and respond
to the text by
answering
the following
questions.

# REVIEW, REFLECT, AND RESPOND

In your own words, how would you explain God as your personal trainer from your own experiences?

_____
_____
_____
_____
_____
_____

What fitness program does God have you on right now? What is He working on in your life?

_____
_____
_____
_____
_____
_____
_____

In what ways has God gotten you into better spiritual shape?

_____
_____
_____
_____
_____

> *However, when He, the Spirit of truth, has come, He will guide you into all truth; for He will not speak on His own authority, but whatever He hears He will speak; and He will tell you things to come.*
>
> *—John 16:13 (NIV)*

*Consider the scripture above and answer the following questions:*

How is this scripture an example of the Holy Spirit as a personal trainer for our spiritual understanding and maturity?

_____

_____

_____

_____

_____

_____

_____

Have you allowed the Holy Spirit to train your hearing? What needs to happen before you can act on what He speaks to you?

_____

_____

_____

_____

_____

_____

_____

_____

In what ways has the devil attempted to take advantage of your weak condition? How has the Word given you the power to resist him?

_____

_____

_____

_____

_____

_____

What does being "guided in all truth" mean? Why is it an essential part of being trained up in the Spirit?

_____

_____

_____

_____

_____

_____

If the job of the Holy Spirit is to train you, what is your job? What should you do with the training?

_____

_____

_____

_____

_____

_____

_____

# YOUR SAFE PLACE

*By continually seeking to live the drenched life,
seeking to be thoroughly covered and completely
filled with the presence of the Holy Spirit, we
are allowing Him to keep us in safe places.*

# REVIEW, REFLECT, AND RESPOND

## READING TIME

As you read Chapter 11: "Your Safe Place" in *Drenched*, review, reflect on, and respond to the text by answering the following questions.

What do you think it means to find safety in Him?

_____

_____

_____

_____

_____

_____

What kind of things does having a safe place rescue or release you from?

_____

_____

_____

_____

_____

_____

_____

Recall a time when you felt the safety of God. What was that experience like for you? What do you remember feeling?

_____

_____

_____

_____

_____

> *When the enemy comes in like a flood, the Spirit of the Lord will lift up a standard against him.*
>
> —Isaiah 59:19 (ESV)

*Consider the scripture above and answer the following questions:*

How do you envision the confrontation depicted in this scripture between the enemy and the Spirit? What images come to mind?

_____

_____

_____

_____

_____

_____

_____

_____

_____

What kind of battles has the Spirit fought on your behalf?

_____

_____

_____

_____

_____

_____

_____

_____

Why do you think you can have peace even when you're under immense pressure? Have you ever experienced this?

_____

_____

_____

_____

_____

_____

_____

_____

What does it look like, in application, to run to your safe space when you are facing adversity?

_____

_____

_____

_____

_____

_____

_____

In what ways does God fight *with* us and not just for us?

_____

_____

_____

_____

_____

_____

# CHAPTER 12

# THE GENEALOGY OF AN OVERCOMER

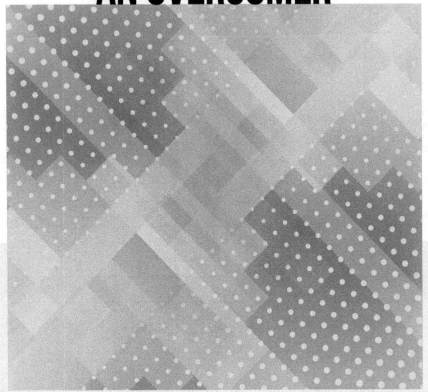

*Is there an overcomer reading this book? Lift up your voice and shout, "NO WEAPON FORMED AGAINST ME SHALL PROSPER!"*

# REVIEW, REFLECT, AND RESPOND

Where in your life are you needing victory?
What do you think God may be speaking to
you about this need?

_____

_____

_____

_____

_____

What does victory look like in the face of
trying circumstances?

_____

_____

_____

_____

How might your battles end differently if
you chose to keep fighting instead of giving
up when it gets too hard?

_____

_____

_____

_____

_____

_____

> *But we have this treasure in earthen vessels, that the excellence of the power may be of God and not of us. We are hard-pressed on every side, yet not crushed; we are perplexed, but not in despair; persecuted, but not forsaken; struck down, but not destroyed.*
>
> —2 Corinthians 4:7-9 (NKJV)

*Consider the scripture above and answer the following questions:*

According to this scripture, why are our physical bodies poor indicators of our destiny as victors in every battle?

_____

_____

_____

_____

_____

_____

_____

What does this scripture tell you about the differences between the suffering of a Spirit-filled Christian and the suffering of an unbeliever?

_____

_____

_____

_____

_____

_____

_____

What can you learn from the biblical characters and their stories outlined in this chapter, and how can you apply those lessons to your own life?

_____

_____

_____

_____

_____

_____

What kind of comfort can you find in knowing many have come before you who have overcome the fight of their lives?

_____

_____

_____

_____

_____

_____

_____

What would victory as an overcomer look like in your current situation? What will you do to ensure you receive it?

_____

_____

_____

_____

_____

_____

Printed in the USA
CPSIA information can be obtained
at www.ICGtesting.com
LVHW010044270124
769490LV00081B/3464